MW00876835

The EDC Bible

1

All Day Carry

EDC Gear, At Your Fingertips™
Flexible Carry System™

By

Chas Newport

This content is copyright of

© NRTFM Ltd 2018

All rights reserved.

ISBN-13: 978-1540711540

ISBN-10: 1540711544

Any redistribution or reproduction of part or all of the contents in any form is prohibited other than the following:

- you may print or download to a local hard disk extracts for your personal and non-commercial use only
- you may copy the content to individual third parties for their personal use, but only if you acknowledge NRTFM Ltd as the source of the material.

You may not, except with my express written permission, distribute or commercially exploit the content. Nor may you transmit it or store it in any other website or other form of electronic retrieval system.

ACKNOWLEDGEMENTS

References to all brand names and trademarks are mentioned under the principle of nominative fair use. I'm not a representative of any brands except NRTFM.com, my publishing company. None of my opinions have been paid for in cash, freebies or favours.

**Once you understand,
you don't need to remember.**

This book is in UK English:

Sceptical of his innocence, they had to analyse the coloured aluminium disc to mount a defence of his behaviour.

- Whenever you see ††† under a picture or in the text it would be a link to an online resource in the eBook. You can still access all those links by going to: ††† **http:// theedcbible.com/wp/links/**

Visual Index Portrait

Landscape view on next page.

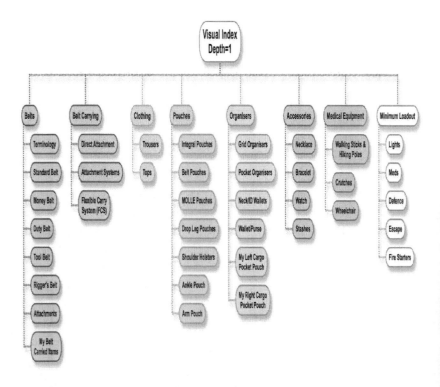

Figure 1 Visual Index Portrait

Visual Index Landscape
You may need to Lock Screen Rotation.

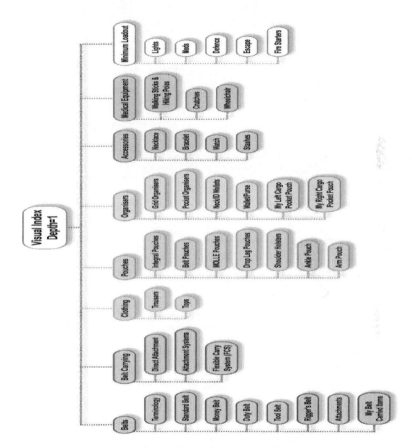

Figure 2 Visual Index Landscape

INTRODUCTION

Let's get a couple of quick things out of the way and get straight to it.

Legal
Know and adhere to the law where you are and everywhere you go or plan to go. Remember: the rules on private property can be much more restricted than in a public space.

Safety

Those of us who practice EDC often carry things which, used incorrectly, can cause injury or even death. Be a role model for the EDC community, don't alarm others and always use tools with skill and care, so you don't harm yourself or others.

No Bag - No Gear

How would you lose your main EDC bag?

- You don't take your bag to the toilet.
- You're near an exit, the fire alarm sounds.
- No bag needed, you're only popping to the shops.
- You left it in the pub while "very relaxed."
- It gets snatched while you're having a coffee.
- Car crash, it's in the luggage compartment.
- Bus/train accident, it's lost during impact.
- You fell through the ice and ditched it.

You'll notice the last few examples are extreme, but that first item is the key. The easiest way to distinguish ADC and EDC is: **The toilet test**. You are at your most vulnerable. If an alarm goes off and you have to rush outside, what do you have? With ADC gear on you, you are never caught "naked" and unprepared. It gives you a solid base of capabilities at your fingertips at all times.

All Day Carry (ADC)

The idea of all day carry is pretty simple. You shift the most useful items from your bag to your body:

- ◆ Pockets
- ◆ Belts
- ◆ Wearables
- ◆ Jewellery

Whatever gender you are, if you carry a bag with 100% reliability, never leaving it unattended, that counts.

Comfort

Items carried all day have to be comfortable. A

key ring rammed to capacity is a great example of how **not** to do it. Splitting them into several smaller **clusters** solves that problem, with the side benefit you can group related keys. We'll show you how to design these rigs and stop them lying in a big lump in your pocket.

Capacity

Splitting things up into multiple rigs also increases capacity and gives you options. If you use a Zippo® you'll know they are very simple and reliable. You'll also know they have a couple of weaknesses. They dry out pretty quickly and they aren't waterproof.

The drying out problem is solved with our rigs because you have plenty of room to carry a canister of fuel and a spare flint.

If you fall into water and need to dry off a "peanut" lighter on your rig is a brilliant backup for your soggy Zippo®. It also dries out very slowly because it has an O-ring sealing the fuel in.

Mobility

How do you move all this gear when changing clothes? The answer is "detachment points" for removing single items, clusters or the whole rig easily. You can quickly move items between clothing, to a different part of your body, your luggage or even a locker.

Security

There are two aspects to security: attachment and visibility.

Our rigs are all designed with an **anchor point** to attach them to your belt, bag or clothing. This is much more secure than lying loose in a pocket where poor pocket design or bad luck can allow it to disappear.

The same structure and distribution we use to enhance comfort and reduce bulk also means items are harder for thieves to see.

Deployment

The final item is deployment. If you organise things into rigs and clusters you can very quickly find the thing you need. Our rigs, combined with pouch and belt items allow you to carry a lot of gear... we hope you have a good memory!

BELTS

Some clothing has internal or external adjusters and no belt loops. They are unsuitable for belt carry techniques but the FCS can still be used with an Anchor Clip attaching it to something you **always** carry.

There are dozens of buckle designs, some designed for appearance and others with a purely functional emphasis. See Appendix A for details. The essentials for us are strength and comfort.

Terminology

Let's use the correct terms for the belt and buckle:

Chape: the clamp or slot which attaches the belt to the buckle.

Mordant: the "bite" or adjustable portion of the buckle.

Prong: the fixed tooth or hinged pin which goes through the hole in the belt.

Tongue: the tip of the belt at the opposite end to the buckle.

Trivia:

The word buckle derives from the Latin word buccula meaning cheek-strap, as for a helmet. You can also see the same root word in the term "buccal swab" in the CSI series.

Standard (Dress) Belt

Duty belts and tool belts are probably overkill for most of us. The riggers belt or a sturdy leather belt 1.5-2.0 inches (38-50mm) wide is a great, low-key choice for ADC. The width and rigidity mean they can support lots of gear and hold it upright. Also be aware that for friction buckles the wider they are, the better they work.

Belt Tail Security

I've lost at least one item (a Zippo Armor plus leather pouch) because I wore it between the last two loops on my left hip. If the tail of my belt slipped through the first loop it could, and did, drop off occasionally at home. Now I use a simple trick to avoid that. **Loosen the belt to its longest position without undoing it.**

Figure 3 Last Hole

You can probably see I've done a slightly amateurish job of shortening this belt and the holes were added using a single hole punch. It's worth investing in one of these if you go on a diet or if the last hole in the belt is a long way from the tip.

Money Belt

This isn't the type of money belt used by market traders and waiters, or the ones you hide inside clothing for travelling. It's a stealth belt for emergencies, looking standard but with a secret compartment on the inside to store an emergency cash stash.

Figure 4 †††<u>Money Belt</u>

While nominally for money you can, of course, within reason put anything into the zipped compartment in these belts providing it is flexible and not too bulky. Try not to put anything in which gives away the presence of the stash because that renders it useless. Also bear in mind you can't get to the contents in a hurry.

Duty Belt

Patrol belts are **not** really designed to hold up your trousers. In fact the presence of bulky duty buckles on either end means it won't fit through even the most generous 2" belt loops. The duty belt goes over your dress belt and should come with a set of "keepers" which clip over or loop around it.

Figure 5 †††<u>Duty Belt</u>

They are amazingly stiff, designed to support a serious quantity of heavy gear like radios, handcuffs, pepper spray, baton, Taser or handgun with ammunition.

For most of us these would not be ADC because they are bulky, snaggy and uncomfortable when sitting. For serious EDC practitioners though they are the ultimate "Bat

Belt" as long as you don't mind taking it on and off.

Tool Belt

These have pretty much the same characteristics as the Duty Belt but usually have pouches for nails and screws and loops for hammers and other tools. Worth a look, but be prepared to take it off when sitting down for long periods.

Rigger's Belt

These are professional safety equipment but that is good news because it means every element is sturdy and of the highest quality.

Figure 6 †††<u>Riggers Belt</u>

They are made of heavy duty webbing which makes a seat-belt look like dental floss. The buckles are chunky steel sliders with a velcro tail anchor. There is always a large steel eyelet under a velcro tab designed for attaching a safety line.

<u>WARNING: Not for Climbing</u>

WARNING: This is an emergency backup in the event of a fall, not a climbing harness. The safety rigging in stadiums and theatres is rigged to stretch, absorbing the fall. Tethering to a rigid infrastructure could result in serious injury.

BELT CARRYING

Let's take a look at the three methods for belt carrying items and assign an abbreviated code (in brackets) for use in the next section.

Tip:

Some chairs have angled corners which create a triangular void behind each of your hips. This is a good place to position bulky items.

Direct Attachment

You can attach some things directly to your belt using integrated clips on the item. That's okay as a temporary measure to free up both hands but isn't ideal when you are moving around stressing the attachment point. I have a SureFire L2 and L4 both of which have clips and we found that they can bend with wear-and-tear.

Attachment Systems

Original Equipment (OE)

The simplest alternative to direct attachment is an Original Equipment (OE) pouch or dock. These are usually well made as the manufacturer doesn't want the accessory to reflect badly on the product.

††† Original Equipment Pouches (OE-S)

††† Original Equipment Docks (OE-D)

Third Party Pouches (TP-P)

If there are no OE attachments for your item there are numerous third party pouches available in all shapes and sizes as an alternative to direct attachment. The best use MOLLE or are at least compatible with the PALS element of it.

†††Third Party Pouches (TP-P)

ALICE

All-purpose Lightweight Individual Load Carrying Equipment was the third iteration of US Army's post war load carrying systems, replacing the 1956 LCE and 1967 Modernised LCE (Load Carrying Equipment). It was replaced by MOLLE in 2003 but we mention it for context and in case you spot any surplus bargains. There is no documented forward compatibility with MOLLE so we advise you to pay a little more for the more contemporary systems.

PLCE

Personal Load Carrying Equipment is a British load carrying system which was invented in 1985 and updated to an improved different "pattern" in 1990 and 1995. It was developed separately from the US systems but both sets were replaced by MOLLE which unified them as NATO standard issue. Again we include for context but advise you to use MOLLE or other compatible systems.

MOLLE

We'll be mentioning MOLLE throughout the book. A slightly mangled acronym for MOdular

Lightweight Load-carrying Equipment. The system was invented in 1997 but not used until 2003. It's aimed at a mainly military audience but there's much to like for fans of ADC and EDC. It was funded with our taxes... we may as well get our money's worth.

Figure 7 †††MOLLE System

The Pouch Attachment Ladder System (PALS) is a horizontal grid of webbing strips, consistent in width and spacing. Vertical straps on pouches can be threaded behind or woven in and out of the horizontal grid on the item you're attaching to. In practice most people don't mention PALS and use the term MOLLE for anything with PALS straps.

PALS

The Pouch Attachment Ladder System (PALS) is a grid of webbing strips, consistent in width and spacing. The straps on the pouch can be threaded behind or woven in and out of the grid on the larger item you're attaching it to.

Figure 8 PALS Attachment

MALICE Clips

Designed in the USA by Tactical Tailor MALICE is a portmanteau abbreviation of MOLLE and ALICE. These simple, robust plastic straps are stiffer and easier to thread than the straps which come sewn onto pouches. They also have a secure catch which won't come undone with inserting a thumbnail or screwdriver tip, unlike the pop fasteners on standard straps.

Figure 9 MALICE 3" and 5"

We've also discovered the 3" straps make ideal loops for attaching MOLLE directly to a 2" belt.

Figure 10 MALICE Belt Loop

MOLLE Sticks

Designed by Vanquest for quick release of pouches like medical packs. Like the MALICE straps, they are stiff and very easy to thread because they are so smooth. A spring loaded clip at the top locks the stick in place by gripping the top PALS strap.

Figure 11 MOLLE StIcks 5"

The locking tabs come threaded with thin, but non-stretching cords you can pull to release the catch. If close together you can tie the cords together so you can pull them both at once. You can drop a pouch in under a second with this technique.

MOLLE D-Rings

OneTigris make good quality MOLLE gear and have a few new ideas of their own. These D-Rings have 360 degree rotation with locks at each position. Take care to engage both sets of barbs, top and bottom of the PALS strap, or there will wriggle loose.

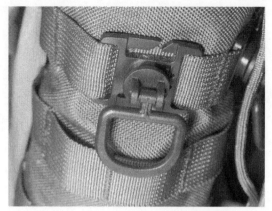

Figure 12 MOLLE D-Rings

ILBE

The Improved Load Bearing Equipment (ILBE) is another upgrade and theoretical replacement for MOLLE but completely backward compatible with it. It was designed by Arc'teryx and manufactured by Propper Inc. Corrects a few criticisms of MOLLE, so worth getting if you can find it.

MAS

The Modular Attaching System from CombatKit is a complete system of packs, vests belts and pouches all from the same source. They are based in Croatia and worth a look if you are based in Europe.

Quality Control

The quality of MOLLE rigs varies widely from minor manufacturing defects to outright knock-offs. There are a few things to check before you remove the labels.

The straps which weave in and out of the ladder system should be double thickness and quite stiff, otherwise they can pull through the later rungs rather than securely locking things together.

The PALS strap must be an exact multiple of the width of the ladder rungs. It's hard to see but in Figure 13 the strap is just too short and the pop fastener too high to go through all the rungs on the bag. It also means there is slack in the strap when connected half a rung short of being taut. That particular annoyance inspired me to write this section.

The rungs on the PALS ladder are generally the right depth and stitched at the correct width even in the fakes but often made from inferior material with coarse stitching and lacking stiffness. Even on higher quality items the outermost loops are sewn into the seam of the item and as a result can sometimes be too narrow to be used due to the bend around the edge.

Third Party Docks (TP-D)

Third party attachment systems like the Peter Jones †††Klick Fast® are aimed at professionals in the military and law enforcement, but there's no embargo on selling them to the public. The various docks, loops and adaptors are perfect for ADC of torches, defence sprays, radios, etc.

†††Third Party Docks (TP-D)

Klick Fast®

Docks

Docks are the core of this system. The plastic one, shown bottom left, threads straight onto a belt. There are three leather loops, one with a similar mounting height to the plastic dock, an extended (shown here on the right) and a double extended. The remaining dock shown here has four holes which can be screwed to a solid surface or pop-riveted through clothing. They even have MOLLE adaptors and one for bike handlebars.

Figure 14 †††Peter Jones Klick Fast® Docks

Each has a wide opening which narrows towards the bottom. In the centre of the narrow part is a flexible plastic nipple which engages with the docking lug on the other half of the system.

Adaptors
The other part of the system is an octagonal lug which clicks into the dock channel. The face with the U-shaped opening allows the equipment to slide in and out of the various docking points without engaging the nipple in the dock. The

other seven sides go under the locking nipple and allow the equipment to be carried securely at various angles. In this context it is ideal for carrying a tactical strobe torch for self defence as it's immediately to hand and quick to deploy. There are specialist attachments for rigid cuffs, batons, cameras, Peli lights and various radio systems.

Figure 15 †††<u>Peter Jones Klick Fast® Octagon</u>

Hands Free

Tip:
As show in figure 16, you can illuminate things while the torch is still on your belt, leaving your hands free.

Figure 16 †††<u>Peter Jones Klick Fast® Tilted</u>

Two-Belt System

If you watch cop shows you will have noticed law enforcement professionals wear two belts. The "dress belt" holds up their trousers and the "duty belt" holds all the cuffs, guns, ammo pouches, etc. What you can't always see is how that system works.

Why?

Comfortable

There's nothing macho about gritting your teeth and continuing to wear uncomfortable gear. At best it's a distraction. The worst scenario is injury ranging from blisters to back injury. Finally anything which pushes you to remove the belt as often as possible is a bad thing.

Light

We can't do anything about the weight or bulk of the items on the duty belt but we can reduce the weight of the additional belt and hardware. We've specified lightweight

Organised

If possible your gear should stay well organised so you don't need to adjust it every time you put it on. It should also be easy to re-arrange items which aren't working efficiently.

Usability

The primary point of doing this is usability. The big downside of direct attachment, even with attachment systems, is having to slide everything off and on when you remove the belt. A good two-belt system leaves most of the gear on the duty belt so you can leave everything on it. You just remove the whole belt when not needed or when changing trousers.

How?

Some people just wear two belts like the cowboys in the movies wore a gun-belt over their standard one. If that works for you that's fine, but you may still want to read on because we think

keepers have many benefits.

If you search for "belt keepers" online you are shown several designs. There are two types, open and closed. The closed ones are designed to secure the loose belt tip and stop items on the belt sliding into a lump. For us the open ones are much more interesting because you can attach the duty belt to the dress belt improving comfort and security.

Hook Keepers

We've done the research and there are several keeper systems with pros and cons. The hook keepers in 17 are light, usable and comfortable.

Figure 17 ††† Hook Keepers

Initially we tried threading the hooks on the

dress belt, open side up so you dropped the rigger's belt in from above. This didn't work well as you still can't removed the belt without removing the hooks, unless the belt loops are huge!

Keepers On Duty Belt

Figure 18 shows the keepers threaded, open side down, on my favourite duty belt, a 4000 pound rigger. They fit the thick webbing and loop tape quite snugly so they don't slide easily, keeping the gear where it is.

Figure 18 ††† Keepers on Duty Belt

Duty Belt On

You don the belt by dropping the hooks over

the dress belt. I try to position the keepers close to the ones on the trousers. The ability to accommodate different belt loop patterns is another upside of this system. You can do the duty belt up relatively loosely so the huge steel buckle is much more comfortable.

Figure 19 ††† Duty Belt On

EDC or ADC?

We've suggested it here because our experience shows a two-belt system is, above all, more comfortable, portable and organised. Whether a duty belt is ADC or EDC is determined by you... when do you wear it? If you frequently take it off it's not ADC.

Flexible Carry System (FCS)™

Carry & Loadout

The final trick is to build your own. Our Flexible Carry System™ (FCS) allows you to carry huge amounts of gear suspended inside your pockets. The FCS forms the foundation of a system for carrying more useful items and rapidly switching them to suit specific tasks, journeys or changes in environment.

The second book, Everyday Carry, follows the same philosophy but uses a different solution. Our Flexible Loadout System™ (FLS) uses pre-defined Kits you can rapidly load into your preferred luggage systems. These Kits are colour coded to identify contents, purpose, durability and safety. We also define some suggested Packs you can pre-load to grab at a moment's notice.

We define some minimal loadouts here and cover a wider range of capabilities and tools in Book 3 Basic Gear.

Levels

Here's the rig, we've split it into three levels:

Anchor Level

The Anchor Level is really simple, it's a loop and a ring. The loop goes onto your belt and the ring acts as the anchor point for the rest of your stuff.

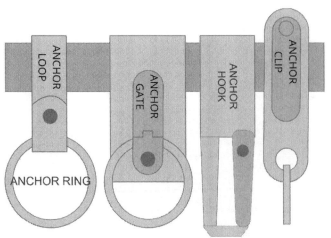

Figure 20 †††Anchor Level

Anchor Level Goals

Physical Security

As the term anchor implies this level requires chunky hardware big enough for a 50mm (2") belt, holding the weight of everything which hangs below it.

The anchor level is potentially exposed to pick pockets so you may wish to consider an <u>Anchor Loop</u> with no gate. A full sized carabiner with a screw-gate, secondary gate or magnetic latch also makes their job a little harder.

Stealth

An alternate approach is to use an integrated gate at belt height, hidden beneath clothing. They can't steal what they haven't seen.

Rapid Re-deployment

You can run a single set of Anchor Level hardware you move from belt to belt. If you can afford it several sets pre-fitted to clothing and luggage is a better idea. That way you can quickly re-deploy your rig at the <u>Load Level</u> in a few seconds by changing to the other anchor.

Anchor Clips

If you decide to use this on your belt or the <u>Pocket Rig</u> you can move it by unclipping and moving the entire thing. You can even hook it into a strap on a rucksack or an equipment vest. The only compromise is that it isn't 100% secure against snagging or lifting.

Figure 21 †††<u>Anchor Clips</u>

Anchor Gates

These are my preferred option because they are compact, cheap and arguably quite attractive. I bought half a dozen to leave threaded onto various pairs of trousers and just unclip the Anchor Ring to move my rig from one to the other.

Figure 22 †††<u>Anchor Gates</u>

Anchor Hooks

All the advantages of the gated variety in the previous section with a lower <u>Detachment Point</u>. Note though the Anchor Ring is at 90 degrees to your thigh when attached it may need a small intermediate ring to flip it.

Figure 23 †††<u>Anchor Hooks</u>

Anchor Rings

These are the simplest solution but require a <u>Detachment Point</u> in the next level down (the <u>Load Level</u>) to allow easy movement. On models with pop fasteners or velcro you can elect to undo the belt loop but that's time consuming and will cause both types to wear out eventually.

Figure 24 †††<u>Anchor Rings</u>

Large Carabiners

A carabiner large enough to thread through a 2" belt is a great solution. They are robust and come with a variety of secondary latches to deter pickpockets. This one has two magnets which click into slots in the gate when it's closed.

Figure 25 †††<u>Magnetic Gate Carabiner</u>

The low tech solution is this twin gate carabiner.

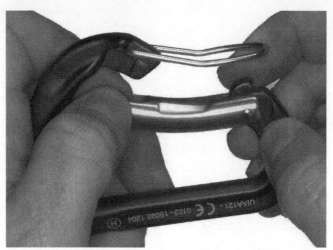

Figure 26 †††<u>Twin Gate Carabiner</u>

Large S-Biners®

Double gate carabiners like the Nitelze S-Biner® will work for narrower belts. Some versions have individual sliding locks or a rotating lock in the centre which locks both gates at once.

Figure 27 †††<u>Large S-Biners</u>

Gear Retractors

If you have an item of equipment you use several times a day like an RFID token or swipe card a high quality gear retractor is an ideal solution.

Figure 28 †††Gear Retractors

Load Level

The Load Level is all about positioning everything for Safety, Security, and Stealth. It is also about Flexibility when you need to move the rig from one deployment to another, let's deal with that first.

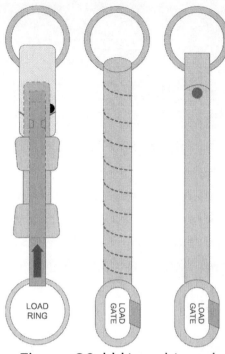

Figure 29 †††<u>Load Level</u>

Load Level Goals

Safety

<u>Snagging</u>

WARNING: Never wear your rigs when operating machine tools or in any situation where snagging may prove dangerous.

Set up all your rigs to minimise the possibility of snagging or damage to clothing and upholstery. This can be tricky in cars with seats which have side bolsters.

Depth

Hip pockets slant to varying degrees. The length of the rig should be set so the lower edge of the Load Ring is inside the pocket slit.

If moving between several pairs of trousers you have two options:

The first is to set the rig to the deepest/most slanting pocket in your wardrobe. The downside of this is that it will almost certainly be too long for some and too short for others.

The second option is to have a Load Level set for each pair of trousers. You need to add a small coupler to the Load Ring so you can move that (rightmost rig in Figure 29) leaving any tether in place.

Stealth

For maximum stealth using a belt anchor you position the rig as far forward as possible so most of the Load Level is hidden. Stealth is compromised when using the Pocket Rig unless you use a very discreet Anchor Clip.

Test all your rigs in a sitting position to ensure it doesn't swing on the anchor and pull itself out of your pocket. This is quite common with heavier gear like CR123 torches and large collections of capsules which can slide easily.

Quick Release Single

These are an excellent choice for trousers with a high cut pocket which doesn't require a tether to lower the Accessories. At around 50mm long they are a perfect combination of tether and Detachment Point.

Figure 30 †††Quick Release Single

Medium Carabiners

A medium sized screw gate carabiner is another possibility. They naturally tend to hang with the narrowest side at the top allowing you to add several <u>Accessory Level</u> rigs if you need to.

Figure 31 †††<u>Medium Carabiners</u>

Medium S-Biners®

Medium S-Biners® are also good and offer a choice of two Detachment Points so you can open the top gate without any risk of losing the Accessories at the other end.

Figure 32 †††<u>Medium S-Biners®</u>

Tethers

Rigid vs Stretch

Rigid tethers are the simplest option but the least flexible and adaptable unless you can find one with a buckle or adjuster.

Stretch tethers are an interesting compromise. They allow you to use things while they are still attached. A great choice for RFID fobs and Smart Cards.

Too much weight though and it loses all the advantages of suspending the Accessories and they'll lie in a heap at the bottom of your pocket.

Tether

This is our recommendation, it is the best of both worlds. The tether based rigs in the diagram and Figure 33 have a Coupler at the bottom to allow easy transfer or detachment of the Accessory Level.

Figure 34 †††<u>Tethers</u>

Accessory Level

The Accessory Level is the bottom end of the rig where all your Accessories are suspended in a neat, flexible array inside your pocket. Medium diameter split rings or cable rings act as the Accessory Loop.

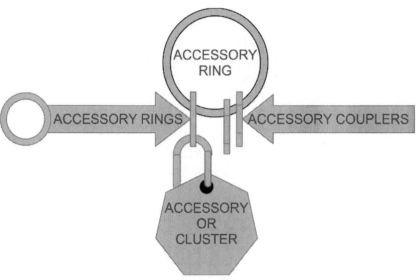

Figure 35 †††Accessory Level

Accessory Level Goals

Deployment

The primary goal is to allow easy detachment of any accessory for immediate use.

Smooth & Flexible

This layer requires physical flexibility because the loads it carries need to fit the contours of your body.

Secondary goals include small size and comfort. The items should take up as little space as possible and be arranged so they fan neatly with the largest and longest in the centre flanked by smaller, shorter ones.

Tip:

Alternating the gates of accessory level couplers lets them nestle together neatly when empty.

Figure 36 †††<u>Alternating Gates</u>

Cable Keyrings

Cable keyrings are an excellent choice because they can bend around your thigh. They are also very thin which means the smaller items threaded on can twist until they are almost parallel. We recommend 1.5mm or thicker and paying decent money... a couple of bucks each not two bucks for ten, you need quality crimping.

Figure 37 †††<u>Cable Keyrings</u>

Quick Release Multiple

These are elaborate and fairly expensive to buy, but if you have a large number of small items they are very well suited to keeping them in a small space. Getting items off is a bit fiddly as they all detach via a single small opening. You have to ensure the item you want is adjacent to that opening.

Figure 38 †††Quick Release Multiple

Ready Made

This ready made cluster by Nitelze® is also excellent. As with the Quick Release above it is best suited to relatively small items of similar size. Also available in stainless steel where the small ones have the central lock shown in <u>Small S-Biner</u>.

Figure 39 †††<u>Ready Made</u>

Lobster Claws

One of the best solutions here is the lobster claw, a micro-carabiner with a spring loaded side gate like the ones in figure 36

Some designs have a rotating barrel which allows the claw to spin to accommodate the load hanging at any angle.

Figure 40 †††<u>Rotating Lobster</u>

Mini Carabiners

Mini carabiners like the one on the left here are cheap and plentiful but are a bit bulkier than the S-Biners® and lack any form of locking mechanism.

Figure 41 †††<u>Mini Carabiners</u>

Small S-Biners

These small S-Biners are the Rolls Royce of secure accessory attachment. The lock makes them trickier to undo one handed or when you're in a hurry.

Figure 42 †††Small S-Biners

Spreaders

Small items like the Photon torches shown here can be clustered together so they don't let lost among larger items. You can also put them in a specific order like Red, UV, White (though I'm intending to mark them with little dabs of paint.)

Figure 43 Spreaders

Detachment Points

Detachment Points (DPTs) are the key to:

◆ Moving Your Rig (Anchor or Load Level)
◆ Using Accessories (Load or Accessory Level)

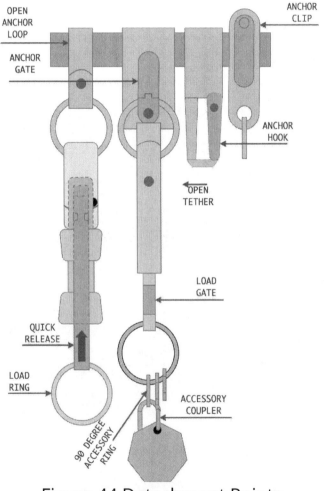

OPEN
ANCHOR
LOOP

ANCHOR
GATE

ANCHOR
CLIP

ANCHOR
HOOK

OPEN
TETHER

LOAD
GATE

QUICK
RELEASE

LOAD
RING

ACCESSORY
COUPLER

90 DEGREE
ACCESSORY
RING

Figure 44 Detachment Points

Tip:

As shown in figure 44 if an accessory is wide and flat you can add a small accessory ring above the coupler to make it lie flat. It is tiny details like this which turn a good rig into an exceptional one.

Depending on your preference you can have one at every level or only one. You should have one near the top of the rig so you can leave the upper part on your belt when you move the rest. Whether you do this at the anchor or load level is up to you. This doesn't apply to the anchor clip which can be moved without removing your belt.

Most accessories can only be used by detaching them. Some rigs can reach a size where using any item while attached to all the others is not possible. That's why I attach all my accessories with couplers of assorted sizes and types.

Long Rig

Finally let's see an overview of the rig in it's entirety.

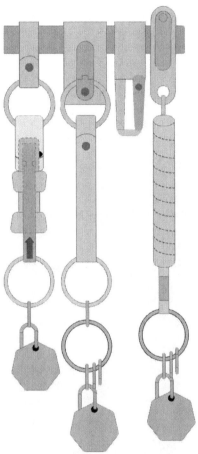

Figure 45 Long Rig

Short Rig

Use the short rig to raise the accessory cluster for shallow pockets or ones where the access is high on the hip.

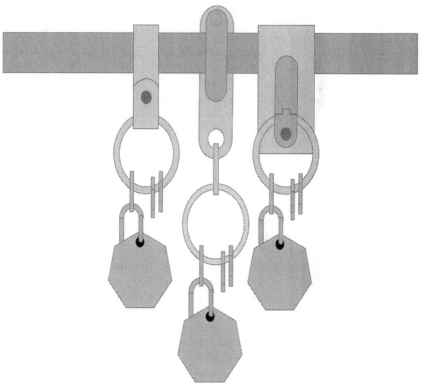

Figure 46 Short Rig

Pocket Rig

Basically one of the Short variants mounted in a pocket. Use it for the following benefits:

- Improved stealth
- Lightness and simplicity
- To avoid snagging

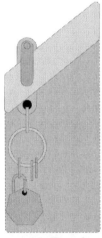

Figure 47 Pocket Rig

This system works best with the smallest Anchor Ring you can get away with as it's at right angles to your body unless you add an extra ring to spin it 90 degrees.

My Rigs

As in the previous sections these are my rigs as I write this, but I'm always experimenting.

Right Hip FCS

This is my right pocket rig; from left to right:

◆ Capsule lighter
◆ Telescopic pen
◆ Emergency meds
◆ Keyring multitool
◆ CR123 Torch

Figure 48 Right Pocket FCS

Below is the rig over the pocket where it lives. Note how all the items have spread across my thigh into a natural fan shape. You should hang the largest, heaviest items in the middle, medium items next with small/thin items outermost.

Figure 49 Right Pocket FCS Exposed

I told you this rig was stealthy. This photo is 100% genuine with all items from the previous photo. I'm not making any effort to stand differently, except to hold my hand back a little.

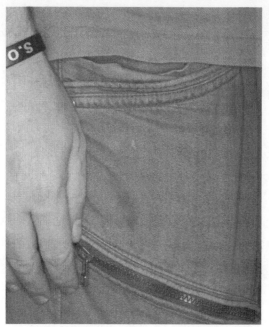

Figure 50 Right Pocket FCS Deployed

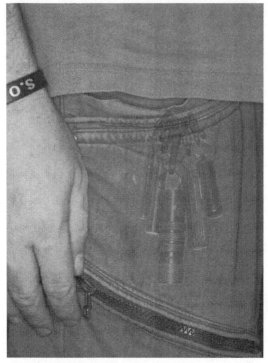

Figure 51 Right Pocket FCS Translucent

Left Hip FCS

This is my left pocket rig; from left to right:

- ◆ Micro scissors
- ◆ Cash Stash
- ◆ Photon Red
- ◆ Photon White
- ◆ Photon UV
- ◆ Keyring Multi-tool

Figure 52 Left Pocket FCS

As before the rig outside the pocket.

Figure 53 Left Pocket FCS Exposed

Again this is 100% genuine, the rig as seen when in situ.

Figure 54 Left Pocket FCS Deployed

If you elect to use the two-belt system we recommend you put the FCS rigs onto the dress belt, not the duty belt. That means they stay ADC when the duty belt is removed. You'll have do use soft leather or velcro anchor points.

CLOTHING

Clothing is one of the most crucial elements in EDC as there is no more certain way to ensure something is near you than by having it in the pockets of a garment you keep nearby, **but "nearby" fails the toilet test.**

The clothing you wear all day is the solution but it has wide requirements which can be compromised by badly distributed gear. You need to be comfortable standing, walking or running. If you work in security full height turnstiles must be considered. When travelling the narrow gangways of public transport and vehicles with seat-belts and airbags must be catered for. You still need to be comfortable sitting in a normal chair with arms.

Trousers

While we encourage you to use the FCS for as much gear as possible it is still impractical for 100% of uses. Slipping stuff in and out of pockets is convenient and a correctly configured FCS rig suspends all items *above* the pocket bottom leaving ample room for a selection of loose items.

Trousers and skirts with pockets are great ADC because social conventions dictate they are quite likely to be at hand all day unless you're a lifeguard. All other clothing is likely to be hung away from you, maybe even in a cloakroom or locker.

Evaluating Trousers

Pockets

This isn't just about having as many pockets as possible. Too few pockets means you have big lumps of gear, but too many adds weight, complexity and may leave you playing "hunt the lump."

The shape of the pockets varies massively. There are some types of "fashion" cargo trousers where the zips and pockets are mostly for show and have odd shapes which look great but aren't any use.

Size is the next element. You probably want one or two large patch pockets for flat objects like notepads, tablet computers or Organisers.

The location of the pockets is really important. If you are planning to put something flat and stiff in a pocket it's no use at knee level. Pockets high on the thigh on the outside can be problematic when you sit down in a chair with arms. Pockets at calf level are out of the way when sitting but if you fill them with anything heavy or noisy they'll drive you crazy, particularly if they are loose fitting.

Tip:

This sounds really geeky but it will pay you dividends to make a list of all your ADC. Plan which parts you are going to carry as ADC in the trousers then map them to the various pockets of the ones you're looking at before you buy...

Some cargo trousers overlay pockets, a patch pocket partially over the pouch of a slit pocket. Bear in mind the contents of the two pockets may interfere with each other in a way which makes them uncomfortable. Leave the labels on until you have tested them with a few things.

Accessibility

Slit pockets seldom have a fastener but sometimes have a flap for looks. Patch pockets almost always have either a fastener inside which passes through the patch, or more commonly a flap over the opening with a fastener on the outside of the patch. There are four principle types of fastener.

Buttons are the most common choice but they have a significant downside. If the flap of a large patch pocket on a thigh is fastened by a *single* button the pocket contents *can* fall out when you are sat down and the patch is horizontal.

Tip:

Avoid "Bobbin" Buttons. Some trousers have a waist fastener shaped like a narrow waisted cotton reel. Avoid these if you carry a lot of gear on your belt because they press into you very uncomfortably under a tight belt.

Pop fasteners are my least favourite solution. Used singly they have the same disadvantages as a button, they can hook on things and come undone very easily and with wear and tear the two section press fit nipples tend to separate rendering them useless. Quality gear often comes with spares but this pre-supposes you have the tools and skills to fit them. Best avoided.

Hook and loop (aka Velcro®) is an excellent choice but noisy to undo if that's a concern for you. If it's a small patch acting like a button this has the same disadvantages as a single button. If it is a *strip* across the whole patch pocket this is a significant improvement over buttons, and pop fasteners. Watch out for the hook side if placing delicate objects into your pocket.

Tip:

If the hook side gets contaminated with fluff you can pinch it off with you fingertips to rejuvenate it. If the loop side goes bald the only choice is replacement.

Zips are the next best thing as they too seal the entire pocket but make sure the zips are good quality. On high quality zips the slider actually has a spring loaded tooth which lifts when you pull the tag and locks it in position the rest of the time.

Cheap zips wriggle undone as you move around. You might perceive metal to be a sign of quality, however, in my experience plastic wins in this application. The teeth are larger, offer lower frictional resistance so they don't jam as often. They resist damage better, don't corrode or rust, don't require lubrication with wax or grease and are easier to deal with if they burst.

Arguably the best known zip maker in the world †††YKK have been making, designing and refining zip structure since 1934. If you buy your kit from a reputable manufacturer using genuine YKK zips it is a mark of quality.

Military Cargo Trousers

Military trousers are the origin of all other styles of cargo trousers. They follow a standard six pocket design: two rear patches with flaps, two hip slit pockets with matching coloured liner, two patches on the outer thighs. The pockets are well placed to allow access while wearing a belt loaded with pouches.

Genuine items have a NATO Stock Number (NSN) and NATO Size Codes. This means you can order items from any source, confident they are built to a specification, not some random definition of Small, Medium or Large.

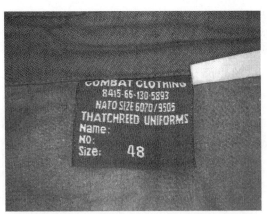

Figure 55 NATO Stock Number

They aren't exclusively in disruptive pattern materials (DPM) and usually come in black, dark blue, grey, khaki, sand and olive green (OG). Also available in at least three weights and weave densities for winter/heavy wear, temperate/medium wear and desert/light wear environments.

The patch pockets have a bellows section to allow them to expand to carry larger amounts of gear or, more likely, bulky field dressings.

Figure 56 †††<u>Military Trousers</u>

The belt loops on these are incredibly robust. They are very deep to accept a 2" Duty Belt or Rigger's Belt, they are also wider for strength, double thickness and double stitched.

Tip:

Pay attention to the position of the belt loops relative to the pockets. You may want to slide a belt pouch along the belt to access a pocket, or move the pouch while sitting.

There is a built in waist adjuster on either side of the trousers. It's two sections of the same thick tape used for the belt loops sewn onto the waistband. The Slide Buckle in the centre lets you adjust by around an inch on each side.

Figure 57 Waist Adjusters

Another feature you won't find on most civilian clothing is drawstrings around the bottom of the trouser legs. Since I'm a bit overweight the inside leg on almost all trousers is too long for me so these are a neat solution. I leave them tightened so I can still get my foot through and leave them done up with a double knot. You can also remove the ties completely leaving a couple of holes at the back as the only clue.

Figure 58 Leg Ties

Cargo Trousers

Most of these have six pockets in similar positions to the military ones but often have hook & loop tabs or zips fastenings. The mil spec trousers avoid these because they can be noisy.

Figure 59 †††Cargo Trousers

Other styles basically add more pockets lower on the legs or overlaid on the six pocket pattern. The hip pockets often have a small "ticket pocket" in the opening. Some have narrow channels or smaller pockets on the patch pockets, ideal for a pen, lip balm or lighter. Pockets tend to be deeper than they are wide and have vertical zips to allow easy access for long objects.

Figure 60 Ticket Pocket

Work Trousers

These are an excellent tip because they have similar designs to the other styles of cargo trousers but often use heavier, ripstop materials like Cordura® either entirely or in patches on high wear areas. Some designs do go a bit mad on pockets.

Figure 61 †††<u>Work Trousers Left Pocket</u>

Some styles have a pouch pocket or two attached at the waist but not sewn around the perimeter so they can move easily when you kneel down, preventing the contents falling out.

Figure 62 †††<u>Work Trousers Right Pocket</u>

Most designs also include slots for knee pads, usually supplied separately, though you need somewhere to carry them when not in use. This means the material has double thickness at the knees.

Tops

You can create FCS rigs for use without a belt. MOLLE is ideal for this as you can fit Anchor Loops through the PALS grid or directly attach a carabiner.

Gilets

Usually pronounced with a soft G like the French name Gilles these are a combination of a waistcoat and cargo trousers. Often sold for hunters or fishermen they are covered in multi-layered pockets. They often have adjustment straps and sometimes D-rings for attaching cord or clipping on items.

Figure 63 †††<u>Gilet Front</u>

They have a logistical downside. The photo is a bit tricky because the colour hides the pockets rather effectively... it's well in excess of a dozen. So many pockets you can lose track of which pocket an item is in. This is particularly true for pockets with others underneath, like an inside pocket with another outside, or a pocket sewn onto another larger one. You can end up playing another round of hunt the lump!

Figure 64 Gilet Poacher's Pocket

Another common feature of these is a deep, wide pocket along the lower part of the back. Referred to as a poacher's pocket it's also a great place to put a pair of over-trousers or even a full set of lightweight waterproofs.

Tip:

You can avoid excess hand luggage charges at the airport by choosing to carry heavier items in your gilet. If you're really sneaky you can unload the lumpier bits from the gilet back into the carry-on.bag after weigh-in.

On a purely practical level you can get hot wearing one of these, even the unpadded ones like the one in figure 63, because they trap an insulating layer of air against your body. Seat-belts can also be problematic as they press things into you when fastened and may even cause injury in an accident.

MOLLE Vest

This is a super-Gilet. The most obvious feature is the <u>PALS</u> system, which allows you to attach dozens of third party patches, pouches, packs and loops exactly where you want them.

Figure 65 †††<u>MOLLE Vest Front</u>

Some models have envelopes on the body called "plate carriers" which allow the fitting of armour plates. Most come equipped with lightweight plastic plates intended for paintball protection but can be fitted with sturdier plates if needed. This does make them heavier than a gilet and considerably stiffer, which causes the vest to move when you sit.

Figure 66 †††MOLLE Vest Back

Going "pouch crazy" will give you a loadout which would be the envy of Batman. Remember, you have to sit in a car at some point and fasten your seat belt...

I confess I'd love to rock one of these but don't have the nerve. They look great on fit, muscular people with properly dangerous jobs, particularly if they are visibly toting weaponry, spray canisters and cuffs. I'm a middle aged author... I couldn't handle the piss taking I'd suffer walking into my local looking like Schwarzenegger in the closing act of the movie †††*Commando*.

Without wishing to seem obsessed remember that for this to be ADC you'll wear it in the loo...

not hung on the back of the door where you might leave it in a panic...

MOLLE Harness

This is an interesting compromise which is lighter, will keep you cooler in hot weather and allows greater freedom of movement. The compromise is that it carries less gear.

Figure 67 †††<u>MOLLE Harness Front</u>

These divide into two styles. The one shown here is basically a wide belt with braces to take some load off the belt. The other style (not shown), the H-harness, has wide, padded shoulders with PALS loops on and one or more crossbars. The crossbars of the H can be a panel of PALS straps you can wear on your chest or back.

Figure 68 †††<u>MOLLE Harness Back</u>

POUCHES

This is the ADC book so, let's be clear, these have to be attached to you, your belt or clothing at all times. They can be attached via PALS to other items in the MOLLE system but if it's not a MOLLE Vest or MOLLE Harness that will usually switch them from ADC to EDC.

Arm Pouch

I've tried arm bands for my phone so it gets a less obstructed signal. The one shown here is also showerproof. I didn't get along with it. By the time I got it tight enough not to slide down it felt restrictive. but plenty of people use them. If you still like wired headphones or ear buds they are a great way to reduce the tangle of wires. Try before you buy.

Figure 69 Arm Band

You can get more generic ones similar to the MOLLE Pouch but you'll only be able to pack light contents like meds , dressings and dried foods or it'll be a nuisance.

Shoulder Holsters

I really like these as a concept and used one for several years until it wore out. In the interim I started carrying a much larger wallet and couldn't find one it fitted into. Now I've switched to a Minimalist Wallet I'll probably start wearing one again.

Figure 70 †††Shoulder Holsters

The Civilian Labs drop leg pouch in the previous section has a shoulder strap accessory for "covert" deployment like this. Covert if you want to look like you have over developed lats... ;-)

Apart from saving your trousers from getting a permanent bulge or pale patch from your wallet I rather suspect these are a bit trickier for pickpockets. If you wear a jacket they are less easy to see, particularly if you carry a decoy in a visible pocket.

Tip:

Muggers Countermeasure: Many of these adjust using pop-fasteners which means it is possible to grab the whole thing by pulling really hard. When you have it set up so it's comfortable sew or glue it permanently.

WARNING: Dragging

Caution: Some thieves are stubborn and strong... they may drag you along, particularly if using a vehicle.

Waist Belt Pouches

Pouches with an integrated waist belt are an inferior choice for several reasons. Firstly, they are awkward to put on if you want to use your belt loops, you have to start at the back of your trousers and go around either side.

The second problem is one of quality. For

some reason many of these integrated belts tend to be thin and narrow with poor quality fittings.

Thirdly, if you wear it without using belt loops you will be forced to remove it when using the loo, failing the toilet test.

Belt Pouches

There are hundreds of non-MOLLE pouches in various sizes and shapes. Multiple small pouches are probably better than a few large ones for flexibility and distribution of weight and bulk. You can use the coloured tagging system described in book two to help you identify the packs you need in addition to your base ADC loadout.

Some pouches have pockets and dividers inside, others are open "dump" pouches but you can put a Pocket Organiser inside them to stop everything collapsing into a lump.

MOLLE Pouches

The straps on the back of a MOLLE pouch are designed primarily for use with <u>PALS</u> but there's nothing to stop you threading a belt through instead. I use all MOLLE pouches, clothing and luggage to maximise the possibilities for creating the perfect rig.

Figure 71 †††<u>MOLLE Pouch</u>

Drop Leg Pouches

You don't have to be toting weaponry or mags to wear one of these, this one from Civilian labs is even in "civvy" colours. It has a flexible attachment system supporting drop leg (belt clip and thigh strap) plus straps for various symmetrical and asymmetrical on-body setups.

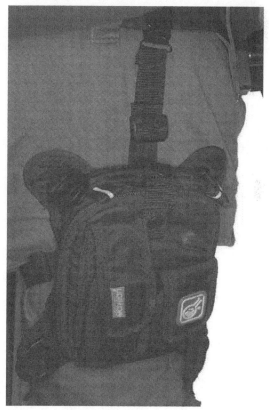

Figure 72 †††<u>Drop Leg Pouches</u>

Ankle Pouch

You don't have to be a cop with a backup "piece" to carry a few items in a wallet or holster attached to your ankle. I am going to assume you are wearing trousers to conceal it.

If you are going to use a decoy or backup wallet strategy this is a great place for your real/backup cash and ID. Make sure you aren't seen accessing it in public though or it becomes a bit pointless.

Tip:

If you use a decoy wallet throw it a few feet away so your attacker has to move away to retrieve it. If possible open up an escape route at the same time.

ORGANISERS

Other than efficient belt carrying these are the most important trick for having lots of useful things to hand. The best ones make things visible so you can find them easily.

There has been an increase in media coverage of street theft from contactless bank cards so it may be wise to consider one with RFID shielding. You can also buy individual RFID envelopes to selectively protect individual cards.

Tip:

If you live in a city like London where they have prepayment cards (Oyster for London) and the ability to pay on-the-fly with a bank card it can sometimes cause issues where a journey is paid for twice. These individual card shields seem a good solution.

Many of these are available in a waterproof version which is another significant gain over carrying things loose in your pockets.

Grid Organisers

Basically a flat card with woven bands of elastic. If that sounds naff it isn't. First the bands are woven asymmetrically so the lengths vary. Second the elastic has exposed rubberised strands which grip things to stop them sliding. These are simple but very, very effective for bags and larger pouches. Too rigid for cargo trouser pockets.

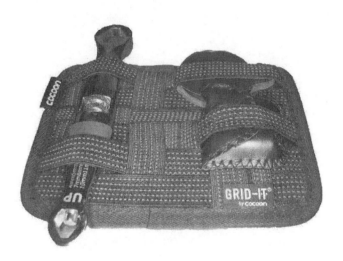

Figure 73 †††<u>Grid Organisers</u>

Pocket Organisers

These are my top-tip for stopping everything falling into a lump in your case, bag or pocket. They are brilliant with Cargo Trousers, indispensable if you need to carry a lot of gear. Basically a slim pouch divided into slits, loops and tubes of varying sizes.

Figure 74 †††Pocket Organisers

These are slimmer than belt pouches and don't have a belt loop, though often have a loop of material to pull out of a pocket easily.

You could even make your own, customising the sleeves and pockets to exactly fit your requirements, cutting exact shapes into a sheet of memory foam with a craft knife. The †††Instructables website has plenty of suggestions for this sort of thing.

Neck/ID Wallets

I use one of these (pictured below) to carry a handful of items:

- ◆ A Bank Card
- ◆ A Few Folded Notes of Cash
- ◆ A Pen
- ◆ A Webbing Cutter
- ◆ An ID Card

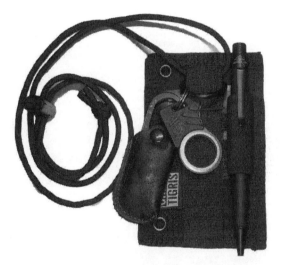

Figure 75 †††Neck Wallets

Confession here: For me this isn't ADC because I only wear it outside the house. That said it's with my coats so I sling it on as I leave, best of both worlds. It provides instant access to everything I need when out and about shopping.

The webbing cutter should still be to hand when hanging upside down in my seat-belt, particularly as I use a sliding titanium collar to keep the neck strap shut.

Tip:
True Story:

I was sceptical of the need for webbing cutters in the real world, but always carried one. My wife was chatting with a colleague who actually found himself trapped upside down in a seat-belt which wouldn't open. Rare but so easily solved, why not? You can cut other things and the edge is shielded so you can take it places a knife wouldn't be allowed (ask first!)

The downside is it's an easy target for muggers as it attracts attention. It can be easily stolen overtly (by threat) or covertly (by cutting the cord). Your assailant could use it as an improvised garrotte by grabbing it. Best used in low risk areas.

Wallet/Purse

There may appear to be a gender divide here. For the purposes of EDC there's little practical difference between carrying a wallet and a coin purse or a purse with partitions for both.

Multi-Purpose Wallet

I used to have two of these (Spec-Ops 'The Wallet'). It has storage for over a dozen cards (more than one per slot), a full length note pocket, full length zip pocket, a small net pouch, internal and external ID windows and lanyard holes. When full they are pretty chunky, impossible to put in a light shirt, blouse or summer trousers.

Figure 76 Multi-Purpose Wallet

Features

Obviously these wallets have several full length slots for high denomination notes in any currency. There is usually a full length zip compartment in one of the slots where you can hide your taxi fare home so you don't accidentally spend it.

Card slots are the next obvious feature. Some are really tight so you can only fit a single card in each one. Others are able to take two or three cards but be careful if you use fewer cards later, they can stretch and loosen the cards.

Some wallets have a netting pouch for a few coins though I use mine for an RFID fob and a jack plug adaptor for aircraft entertainment systems.

Mine has two ID windows, one outside and one inside.

Ones with outside ID windows often have two holes sized for paracord with a single knot.

These wallets are unsuitable for dress jackets, and very visible in cargo trousers... which I think is why one of mine was nicked.

Tip:

If you aren't operating multiple wallets you have "all your eggs in one basket"... lose this you lose everything.

Altogether they are a pretty poor solution. One of mine was my "stunt wallet" stolen by a pickpocket with only twenty Euros, my passport and a single card in it. I'm oddly attached to my remaining one. As a result of thinking about this I'll probably change to using several smaller things instead and use the big one as a *proven* decoy...

Minimalist Wallet

These are at the other extreme. Not much more than a bundle of cards in a fancy elastic band but they are really elegant. A lot of stuff in the smallest possible space... the essence of efficient, effective ADC. This one has a capacity for 12 cards and a good wad of folding. There's a small pouch for a few coins or some memory modules.

Figure 77 Minimalist Wallet

This is the perfect partner for the <u>Decoy Wallet</u> technique as even the most skilled thief is more likely to notice the decoy than this tiny lump. Particularly if the decoy is the Multi-Purpose wallet stuffed with dummy/trashed cards and low denomination cash bulging a back pocket.

Coin Purse

These broadly fall into three styles: the organiser, the pouch and the tray.

Organiser

The emphasis here is on rapid access to the currency inside. These fall into two types: rigid plastic or metal, ones with springs for the coins and leather/plastic ones with lots of compartments. The rigid ones are not appropriate for us but the soft versions maybe be of use, they are big though.

Pouch

This doesn't have to be a drawstring pouch like something out of a historical drama. The pouch shown here has a side zip. It's so hefty I'm slightly worried my wife will be arrested for carrying an offensive weapon. It works well. You lie it in your palm, unzip it and pick out what you need.

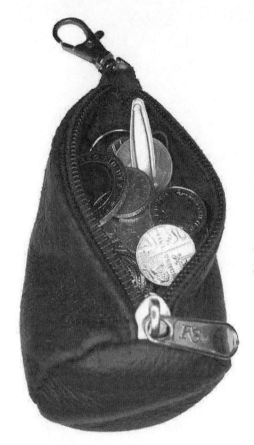

Figure 78 Pouch Open

Tray

Trays go a step further giving you a large, flat space to spread the coins around so you can pick them over. The catch on this one is a neat magnetic one which self centres.

Figure 79 Coin Purse Open

Customisable

The Tamrac system is an interesting halfway house with movable partitions built in. It's a far better solution than making your own as the materials are of a very high quality.

My Left Cargo Pocket Pouch

- ◆ Zippo Fuel Canister
- ◆ EDC Pliers (Generic)

Figure 80 †††<u>My Left Cargo Pocket Pouch</u>

My Right Cargo Pocket Pouch

- True Utility Torch/Laser Pointer
- Chapstick (with UV protection)
- Micro SD to USB Adapter
- 2 x USB Sticks
- Diamond Whetstone

Figure 81 †††<u>My Right Cargo Pocket Pouch</u>

ACCESSORIES

One of the easiest ADC tricks is to maximise the usefulness of ordinary objects. A good way to do this is combining form and function. Necklaces and bracelets are a perfect opportunity to sneak in some extra features and watches are full blown wrist computers now.

Necklace

Rather than hanging something purely decorative around your neck why not dangle something useful. As you'll see it doesn't have to be ugly to be useful.

Dog Tags

If you are a perfect specimen of health these are a really cheap way of passing basic information to first responders if you are unconscious. However, if you take meds daily, have allergies, or have ongoing medical conditions pertinent to your treatment, the SOS Talisman is a far better solution.

SOS Talisman

The SOS Talisman isn't going to save your life in the field, but if you're unconscious when help arrives it could. Inside is a tiny strip of folded hexagons of a paper-like but damp resistant substance. It has details like:

- Name
- Address

- Holiday Address
- Phone Numbers
  - Next of Kin
  - Doctor
- Date of Birth
- Allergies
- Medications

Figure 82 †††SOS Talisman

Tip:

Make sure you use an indelible ink so it doesn't run if it gets damp, the capsule is sealed but it may not be opened under ideal conditions.

If you have access to an old typewriter with a ribbon they are great for this as the strip comes as a sheet with tear off sides. You can feed strip longways through the carriage with care. Failing that use an indelible pen with a fine tip.

Emergency Meds

Another practical choice is a cylindrical capsule you can carry a variety of things in. These are a bit more bulky than the SOS Talisman but obviously more spacious. Titanium is the best choice if you can afford it. It's tough, lightweight, corrosion resistant and hypoallergenic, brass is also good as it is hard and machines well.

Figure 83 †††<u>Emergency Capsule</u>

I haven't seen this mentioned elsewhere but where rescue might take 12 hours or more there are many conditions which can be fatal without medication. You could have a vast knowledge of survival techniques but die anyway for the lack of a few pills... now that, Alanis, is Ironic!

Figure 84 †††<u>Emergency Meds</u>

So my top suggestion for these is medication. I carry 24 hours worth of meds with me at all times and add more when on holiday. I've frequently used the evening dose when we've been delayed returning from a day or evening out.

Some meds shouldn't be exposed to air and should be left in a carefully trimmed blister pack. All meds should be refreshed well before their expiry date so it's easiest to change them all at once based on the one with the shortest shelf life.

Fire Steel Necklace

This †††<u>ferro rod necklace</u> is true genius. A paracord adjuster made from a hard ferrocerium variant and a disk shaped striker. You don't get the long stroke of the longer, purpose made rods but this is a last ditch item. If you have to ditch your other gear because it's dragging you down, you still have this. You still have a chance.

Figure 85 †††Fire Steel Necklace

Bracelet

A bracelet is another item where you can elegantly combine form with function.

SOS Bracelet

With the emphasis on form there is a bracelet equivalent of the <u>SOS Talisman</u> described earlier, available in everything from solid gold to titanium.

Paracord

Turning to a primary goal of function, you'd have to have lived off planet for the last few years not to know about paracord bracelets. What you may not have seen is the increasing number of things they are hiding in the clasps or woven into the cord.

Figure 86 †††<u>Paracord Bracelet</u>

- Whistle
- Compass
- Firesteel & Striker
- Steel Shackle
- Fish Hooks
- Line
- Safety Pins
- Floats
- Shot

Watch

The number of wrist computers covering all the bases for survival is increasing. You can get everything from a compass to a distress beacon.

There are three schools of thought here:

- Mechanical (Self Winding)
- Quartz Crystal
- CPU Clocks

Smart Watches

Smartwatches certainly have apps for all the basic EDC needs as long as you get one with a compass sensor as a bare minimum but most seem to go much further and have GPS. Some even have barometers and heart rate monitors... but it all comes at a price... battery life! Though even here things are improving with the Casio †††Smart Outdoor Watch WSD-F10, which they claim can last a week on a single charge.

†††Smart Watches

We cover powering devices in the field in one of the other books in this range so it's possible. Buying a watch with a battery life in months or years with a solar cell built in is one less thing to worry about.

Casio Pathfinder

The Casio Pathfinder range is an excellent choice combining low power consumption with built-in solar charging. They are rugged, waterproof to decent depths and even have motion triggered back lights.

Figure 87 †††Casio Pathfinder

Inspect the feature list to make sure you get the most bang for your buck, look out for:

- Compass
- Barometer
- Depth Gauge
- Radio Controlled Worldwide Automatic Time Setting
- Solar Power
- 100m+ Immersion

Garmin Vivoactive

Everyone knows Garmin as a major player in handheld GPS so this is the central feature of all their wrist tech.

†††Garmin Vivoactive

They have a range from large rectangular devices with huge screens to watches with round and square dials. If you need accurate height readings to orient yourself on a map then GPS will always be more accurate than the pressure based sensors in most other devices.

Suunto

Suunto take a different approach by making the battery really easy to change using only a coin to twist open the battery hatch. Carry a few spares in one of your pouches and you're set.

†††<u>Suunto</u>

The basic features for survival are well covered with a compass and a barometer which includes a storm warning. Cleverly they use motion sensors to detect movement and switch the pressure sensor to gauge changes in pressure as height rather than weather.

Victorinox

This flagship brand in multi-use tools has expanded into watches, one of which has a nifty built in compass. While lacking many of the features of the other watches here it is also considerably smaller.

†††<u>Victorinox</u>

Trivia:

Founded in 1884, the company was renamed for the founder's late Mother Victoria in 1909. The compound name Victorinox (Victoria-Inox) came about in 1921 with the introduction of "acier inoxidable" - stainless steel, into the product range.

Stashes

Stashes are stacks of coins or tightly folded notes for use in an emergency. I carry two of these, a coin one on my car keys and one with a folded note on my keyring.

Coin Stash

Coin stashes are great for parking change, depending on your currency they can be a bit bulky and heavy. Mine has five £1 coins and I have to take care which way up my folding ignition key goes in the ignition or the weight folds it.

Figure 88 †††<u>Coin Stash Open</u>

Upside: really neat and organised. Downside: usually only one kind of high denomination coins. If it annoys you as a key fob slip it in a car door pocket or centre console as emergency parking change.

Note Stash

The note stash is much more practical as a single middle value note like a UK £20 is tiny when folded correctly. If all the notes in your currency differ in colour rather than size, you're laughing, but don't put in something so large a small shop or taxi driver might not have enough change.

Figure 89 †††<u>Cash Stash</u>

MEDICAL EQUIPMENT

I've included this as ADC because those with a permanent medical need for these items will pass the toilet test with ease.

Almost all equipment of this kind is either aluminium or carbon fibre which means they are hollow. That gives you a sizeable compartment in which to store all manner of emergency medical supplies, tools etc.

Consider putting the items into a pouch or capsule with a loop of strong thread to assist in easy retrieval. You can trap the thread in the end cap of the hollow part or stick it to the inside with a strip of PVC tape.

Walking Sticks & Hiking Poles

These items are always in two or three sections separated by an adjuster collar which twists. This adjuster can be slackened to completely release the lower sections of the pole. Remember to mark the current height with a piece of PVC tape or note it from numbered markings on the stick beforehand.

Aluminium trekking poles are lightweight but have a weakness, literally, if damaged, as any dent in the structure makes them unusable.

Carbon fibre is lighter, stiffer and more resilient to impact than aluminium. The only downside for ADC is that the walls are thicker and internal voids are smaller.

†††Walking Sticks/Hiking Poles

When you are dealing with two sticks or crutches it is vital the weight is evenly distributed unless you have a pronounced difference in strength between one side of your body and the other.

Crutches

With crutches the tubes are really large so you need to take care not to put so much weight in that you cause more problems than you solve. Access may be a problem, I haven't had a chance to see one close up... by all means email me with your experiences. I'm just putting it out there...

Wheelchair

If you are a wheelchair user you have an opportunity where ADC is concerned. Your chair will usually have the option of various accessories for carrying equipment, groceries, etc. As with crutches and walking sticks you can conceal a few emergency items like cash or back-up meds inside the hollow tubes to be retrieved in an emergency.

The same pouches and organisers used for cargo trousers and rucksacks will enable you to store and locate huge amounts of gear in the side and rear pockets of your trusty steed.

MINIMUM LOADOUT

We'll cover what to carry in greater detail in book three, but here is a short list of items we think are essential if you want to be ready. I've listed them roughly in order of likelihood but you should carry all these if possible. The letters in brackets are the recommended carry method for each.

Lights

Finding yourself in the dark is one of the most likely scenarios where ADC can deliver benefits. Torch intensities range from a small glimmer to a piercing beam of blinding intensity. Uses include:

- Obstacle Avoidance
- Emergency Signalling
- Area Lighting
- Weapon Targeting
- Self Defence

Tactical (OE/TP-D)

Strobe Mode

Don't confuse strobing with flashing, For our purposes we'll define strobing as a frequency of 10Hz (flashes per second) or over. Factory strobes are limited to 10-12Hz to minimise the risk of triggering epilepsy which *mostly* occurs due to prolonged exposure (90 seconds) above 15Hz.

Arguably the greatest advantage of strobe

lights over guns, knives, conducted electricity weapons (CEW) and sprays is the ability to affect multiple targets.

The range of these lights is far beyond the fifteen feet commonly quoted for civilian CEWs and also considerably greater than even the most powerful pepper sprays used for bears and other large animals.

WARNING: Epilepsy

WARNING: Strobes can cause epilepsy with no prior history.

Even people not susceptible to epilepsy will be disoriented by stroboscopic lights. The brightness of the flashes will cause visual disturbance by saturating the retina causing brief depletion of the chemical triggers in the eye. That strange green cast or spot you get if a bright light shines in your eye is caused by this. When the light source is removed, particularly in subdued lighting, the affected parties will have difficulty seeing for tens of seconds.

While active the repeated flashing causes dizziness and a loss of balance. I've experienced this first hand with a laboratory strobe some distance away and had difficulty walking in a straight line. If I had been exposed at close range I think the effect would have been much larger and I'm certain it would give a user time to leave the area.

Adjustable Brightness

The latest generations of Xenon arc and LED lights are extraordinarily bright. It is, therefore, essential you buy one with adjustable brightness for the preservation of your night vision.

Adjustable brightness is also an energy saving measure but only in LED based torches. LEDs need a voltage of around 3v to work so you can't cut the voltage like a dimmer (rotary resistor) does with an incandescent bulb. LEDs use a device called a pulse modulator to very rapidly flash the LED decreasing the net amount of light per second and using less energy. Incandescent lights cycle too slowly for this method.

Pencil Beam

A pencil beam is useful as, by definition, it improves "throw" or range because most of the energy is being focussed into a narrow column. Some tactical weapon lights have a pencil spot for crude aiming and a disc (or corona) for target acquisition.

While it lacks the disorienting effects of a strobe, a bright light still has the effect of dazzling an opponent, making them squint and ruining their night vision.

Flood Beam

A flood beam should provide even lighting over a large area, preferably while relatively close by, so you can adjust it as you work.

Tip:

Parabolic reflectors control the beam shape, broad, narrow or narrow with a corona. Parabolas only have one ideal focal point where the emitter must be. Torches with "zoom" generally break this rule creating a void in the beam pattern. Buy two dedicated torches or one torch with two emitters/reflectors.

Last Ditch (FCS)

Slow Flash/SOS

Slow flashing is a combination signalling and battery saving measure. Flashing or moving light sources naturally attract more attention than steady, stationary ones. As described earlier, turning the light source off some of the time saves battery... in this instance this applies equally to LED and incandescent.

Adjustable Brightness

Adjustable brightness in your last ditch light is primarily to extend the battery life as most use small "coin" style batteries. With the rising efficiency of LEDs these can flash for hours or even days, extending your opportunity for rescue.

Meds

Pill Stash (FCS)

Many of us suffer from high blood pressure and other ailments where lack of daily meds can be a serious, even fatal hazard. It therefore makes sense to carry at least 24 hours (maybe even 48 hours) on you at all times. There's no point knowing how to survive an emergency if you're going to die from lack of something so easy to carry. A sealed high quality capsule like the one in figure 84, attached to an FCS rig, is the perfect solution (can also be worn as a pendant).

Epinephrine Autoinjector (EpiPen®)

(OE/TP-S)

Obviously if you suffer from anaphylaxis (allergic reaction to stings and injections) carrying Epinephrine Autoinjector, often known by the trademarked brand name EpiPen®, is essential.

Try to get a purpose made pouch or use one of the generic torch pouches with a belt loop so it's with you at all times.

Defence

Legal

What you are allowed to carry for self defence varies widely from country to country and often within countries due to state laws or private ownership. We therefore recommend you carry something that's legal in as many environments as possible.

The aim is to temporarily disable or disorient an attacker just long enough to get away. Even if your laws allow lethal force, if the assailant is unarmed it may aid your defence if you use a lower level of violence as a first response.

Sprays (TP-D)

The usual legal health warnings apply. Be aware of local law at the country, state, county and private property levels. Know your rights with respect to defending yourself and what constitutes reasonable or proportionate force.

Some countries allow the use of irritant sprays

like CS and pepper sprays. Others, like the UK, only allow the use of non-irritant dyes and siren devices. The purple canister shown below is called Trident Spray®, it has a foul smell, indelible skin staining UV dye and a 130dB air siren.

Figure 90 Defence Spray

The Klick Fast® system described earlier has a specific attachment for irritant chemical sprays. It comes with several canister holders including 35mm and 38mm. The holder slides into a rail on the dock and is held in place by a pop fastener which makes it very quick to deploy. The strap is very thick and rigid preventing accidental triggering. The holder is tethered to the dock to keep it attached if dropped during a struggle. The combination of these features makes third party docking systems our preferred carrying method.

Escape

The need for these may seem unlikely but car accidents and public transport breakdowns are among the more likely scenarios you should be prepared for. If you include the likelihood of needing to assist someone else the probability rises considerably. My wife's boss found himself upside down in a jammed seat-belt... that's close enough for me.

From Vehicles (FCS)

The tool on the left is a combination webbing cutter and glass breaker. We've removed the quick release keyring loop so you can see the well concealed blade which does the cutting. The cylinder at the top is a spring loaded centre punch for breaking toughened glass.

Figure 91 Escape Tools

The tool shown on the right in figure 92 is only a webbing cutter. You could use it for everyday parcel opening etc, but then it may not be razor sharp when needed.

From Rooms/Buildings

At the risk of appearing to be obsessed by toilets I'm going to use another loo based example here. During the Victorian era here in the UK they made things properly. Toilet "cubicles" made from 10mm of chipboard with a six inch gap for weirdos to shove a mirror under did not exist. Some of our older pubs still have properly built toilets. The walls are made from shiny engineering brick or tiled from floor to ceiling, all sealed with a full-length door. The locks are over a hundred years old. If one of these comes off in your hand you need a tool to unscrew the lock case and remove the bolt.

Penknife (OE/TP-S)

We'll go into a detailed analysis in book three but we all know the elephant in the mountains is the Swiss Army Knife (SAK). It's the Swiss Army

Knife of penknives. Nothing crams more into a small space than these and while ergonomically awkward in some cases none of the tools have been compromised to the point of being unusable.

Multi-Tool (OE/TP-S)

Just a quick word on terminology... sorry. There is absolutely no consistency over spelling, you'll find "multi tool", "multi-tool" and "multitool" in current use. To add to the confusion there's an oscillating power tool called a multi-tool too. This means you have to add a brand name to narrow things down then rely upon your search engine to deal with the synonyms.

Time for another quick legal reminder. Here in the UK we have ridiculous knife legislation at the time of writing. I won't bore you with the details but in a nutshell blades must have a spring loaded slip-joint like the SAKs. No blade locks allowed. Since these are a common feature on multi-tools you need to buy a blade-less version or one without locking blades.

Fire Starters

A lighter is another item you can carry which has multiple uses from a direct source of light and heat to an ignition source for a camp fire.

You have two choices here, high-tech or low-tech. There is a new generation of flameless, windproof rechargeable lighters. They are only useful as an ignition source.

The low tech solution is the good old fashion liquid fuelled lighter. Butane lighters burn hotter but replacement fuel is bulkier and arguably more dangerous as it's stored under pressure. The liquid fuelled lighters like the Zippo® can be refilled from a small purpose built tank. During post war rationing my Dad used to refill his by dangling it into a truck fuel tank on a string! DO NOT TRY THAT!

Main: Zippo® (OE)

The old fashioned liquid fuelled lighters like the Zippo® are the most versatile. The distinctive yellow flame generates plentiful visible light which the other technologies do not.

The flame is cooler than butane but perfectly adequate for lighting tinder. The chimney designs do make them resistant to all but the strongest winds, particularly when used in the lee of your body. You can even use them as a crude hand warmer by burning the flame for a few seconds with the lid partly closed before clicking it shut and cupping it in your hands. Practice this carefully somewhere safe so you don't burn yourself in the field.

The final advantage is easy refuelling. I'm utterly sick of trying to figure out which one of the little adapters is correct using trial and error. You can't tell when the lighter is full until butane sprays all over the place with a smell like a frozen fart. And you're never sure if it's actually because the adaptor is wrong. And I hate throwing away half full butane cylinders because the built in nozzle has split.

Another disadvantage of other lighters is all the shapes and sizes, you can't get a snug fitting belt pouch for most models. The Zippo® range on the other hand has a vast range of pouches and even a quick release frame. The one below has a sturdy stitched belt loop and a notch to push the lighter out.

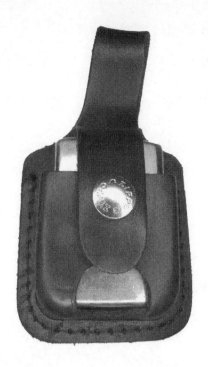

Figure 93 Main: Zippo® (OE)

I prefer the Zippo Armor® as the 50% thicker case has a chunky feel and makes a satisfying clunk when you open it.

You should always carry at least one spare flint in the plastic dispenser or hidden under the wadding in the base (or both). The only downside of the design is the lack of lid seal which means they gradually dry out. Spare fuel in the sealed refill cylinder is, therefore, very sensible.

Backup 1: Peanut Lighters (FCS)

These are a brilliant backup to your main lighter. Always buy one with an O-ring inside the lid as this overcomes the only really disadvantage of the Zippo and its various imitators... it stops it drying out.

Figure 94 Backup 1: Peanut Lighters (FCS)

Backup 2: Keyring Fire Steel

(Ferrocerium Rod)

These keyring steels aren't as long or as thick as the grown up ones. The stroke is shorter and they won't last forever but they are perfect for an ultimate fallback.

Drowning is the second most common cause of death in the wild, with falls at number one. Keep these backups together as an Emergency Fire Kit on a separate dedicated rig. If necessary you can dump everything else at the top detachment points. You still have a way to warm yourself up when you reach dry land.

Figure 95 Emergency Fire Kit

Water

Main: Personal Filter

Personal filters come as thick straws or cylinders about 6 inches long. The cylinders are bulky as an ADC item but a good pair of cargo trousers or the ruler pocket of some work trousers will easily hold the straw style . The benefits are well worth it.

My kit also has a rubber adaptor for "back flushing" when a tap with clean water is available. This extends the life of the filter. I use a LifeStraw® which will process up to 1,000 litres. It has an auto shutdown feature for safety.

Figure 96 †††Main: Personal Filter

These filters do not guarantee the result will necessarily taste like tap water. Their sole purpose is to make the water drinkable. Some systems have a filter stage specifically aimed at improving flavour, or lack of it.

Backup: Purification Tablets

Tablets produce between one litre and twenty litres of drinkable water. So hundred tablets will treat as little as 100 litres of water and as much as 2,000 litres. Read the instructions carefully. Some pills will leave a distinct "swimming pool" flavour in the water, but you just have to put up with it.

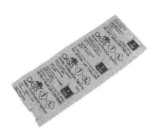

Figure 97 †††Backup: Purification Tablets

The best tablets also remove suspended dirt.

Some fine particles will not clear, no matter how long you wait. They may not be toxic but make drinking it less pleasant.

THANK YOU!

Thanks for buying our book. We hope it will help you. If you do have an adventure where our ideas helped please get in touch at ✝✝✝ TheEDCBible.com.

Cheers, Chas & Sooz

Advanced Review Copy List

If you want to help out and get free books in return, you can join our ARC team. ARC = Advance Reading Copy. Basically an early draft of the book for you to read and comment on if you wish to. You are not obliged to buy the book or review it when it comes out, but it would be great if you chose to. You'll get to see the finished product you helped create.

†††**Join our ARC Team!**

Launch Discount List

If that seems a bit much, how about a sneaky heads-up for a huge discount at book launches?

†††️ **Join the Launch Discount List!**

The EDC Bible 2: Flexible Loadouts

Our Flexible Loadout System (FLS) Pre-defined Kits for quick selection appropriate for your task, duration, weather and other variables.

- ◆ Dynamic loadouts.
- ◆ Quick pack load or reload.
- ◆ External identification.
- ◆ Fast location & deployment.

†††**http://books2read.com/EDCBEveryDayCarry**

The Rusty Nut Bible

Don't reach straight for your longest spanner... Our systematic 10-Step freeing system starts gently, gradually escalating to destruction as a last resort.

- ◆ Minimise shearing risk.
- ◆ Preserve fasteners & irreplaceable parts.
- ◆ Avoid injury through excessive force.
- ◆ Save money discarding fixable gear.

†††**http://books2read.com/TheRustyNutBible**

Fall Asleep in 60 Seconds Gadget

Edition

- ◆ Trouble falling asleep?
- ◆ Keep waking up?
- ◆ Tired in the mornings? Bad Tempered?

You may be suffering sleep poverty. I had the same problem and needed a solution. I am happy to share what I found

- ◆ A Simple, complete, drug free solution
- ◆ ... and gadgets to assist

††† **http://books2read.com/ FallAsleepIn60SecondsGadgetEdition**

PLEASE LEAVE A REVIEW

We're a tiny independent publisher.
The Industry is dominated by giants.
Please help us stand out.
Most people won't buy things with no reviews.
If you haven't left one already, please leave a review!
This will take you to your preferred store:
†††**https://books2read.com/EDCBAllDayCarry**

APPENDICES

Appendix A Buckles

The buckle makes a huge difference to comfort, adjustability and security. Comfort is a particular problem if, like me, you are carrying a bit of extra weight. Large buckles can be extremely uncomfortable when sitting down, even for short periods. They divide into several distinct mechanisms.

Friction

Friction buckles use teeth or textured rollers to prevent the belt from moving. All designs exert greater force when more force is applied to the belt.

Toothed

Toothed adjustable buckles are seen mainly on

fabric belts because the teeth inside the buckle need to grip the material when flipped shut. The belt pulling on the teeth pulls it shut more so security is good.

Figure 98 Toothed Adjustable

Make sure the metal of the buckle is thick or the teeth will bend and the belt will fail. The downside of this design is that the material eventually begins to fray as the teeth always fall on the same area.

Slide Buckle

The Slide Buckle has a frame with a sliding bar across it. The belt passes around the bar and back under the leading edge of the frame. As the bar slides along the frame it clamps the belt and the more you pull, the firmer it grips. Shown here on a Riggers belt...

Figure 99 Slide Buckle

Webbing belts, which can be slippery with this style of buckle, often use a large patch of velcro to secure the tail of the belt so it can't move. Hook and loop tape is designed to be weak when pulled apart but immensely strong when pulled sideways. The Rigger's Belt using 4000lb webbing uses this style of buckle.

Ramp Buckle
This is a similar mechanism to the slide buckle but uses a hidden pin running in a curved slot. You thread the tongue through the buckle and

pull the pin up the arc with your finger and thumb so it squeezes the belt.

Figure 100 Ramp Buckle

Double D-Buckle

This friction based mechanism only has two moving parts, two D-shaped rings. The tongue goes through the centre of both Ds then comes back sandwiched between them. Pulling the belt closes the gap between the Ds, binding the belt.

Figure 101 Double D-Buckle

This is a really simple, comfortable, secure system. It is also infinitely adjustable.

Prong

Prong buckles are the most common. In these designs a prong passes through a hole in the belt. There are two styles.

Prong & Frame

The hinged prong is the type we are most accustomed to. The belt passes through a frame and the prong passes through one of the holes in the belt, preventing it from sliding back.

Figure 102 Prong & Frame

Upsides are simplicity, strength if the prong and belt are thick and ultimate security, there's no way this can come undone accidentally. The only downside is adjustability which is incremental based on the distance between holes.

Plate Buckles

The plate buckle is a simple rectangular plate. The mordant is a short curved tooth sticking out of the back, which hooks directly through one of the holes in the belt.

These are very neat in appearance and very comfortable. The uncluttered front provides a large area for creative and attractive designs if that floats your boat. The only downside is that it isn't as secure as the others, any release of tension can cause the tooth to come free and that's it, open.

Latch/Catch

Duty Buckle

Duty buckles are designed for security so two hands are required to remove them. The main clasps work like a rucksack where you squeeze both sides with your finger and thumb.

Figure 103 Duty Buckle

The secondary release is usually a button through a hole in the buckle which needs to be pressed at the same time, usually with the other hand. Adjustment is infinite, usually simple hook-and-loop threaded through and doubled back through either side of the buckle.

Hook & Catch

Hook and catch belts where a hook on one half engages with a recess on the catch side were historically very popular on nurse or military uniforms but have been largely superseded by superior designs. Like plate buckles a momentary release of tension can undo these, they are also a pain to adjust because adjustment isn't built into the buckle system.

GLOSSARY

MOLLE
MOdular **L**ightweight **L**oad-carrying **E**quipment

PALS
Pouch **A**ttachment **L**adder **S**ystem
MOdular **L**ightweight **L**oad-carrying **E**quipment
Pouch **A**ttachment **L**adder **S**ystem

BACKMATTER

Acknowledgements

The author is not a representative of any brands mentioned. This book relies on the principle of nominative fair use. He acknowledges the true ownership of any and all trademarks referred to in the text.

I'd like to thank my wife Sooz for her continued patience regarding my new career. Thanks also to all my beta readers for spending hundreds of hours proofreading my stuff. Any remaining errors are my cat walking across the keyboard after the corrections :-)

Image Attribution

I do not believe in stealing or taking credit for other people's work and have made every effort to acknowledge the work of others where I've used it as is or as a derivative work.

Below are links and license details for all the images I have used in this book not created by me. I have tried to use material which is free to use as I can't afford royalty fees at this stage in my career. If I have broken the terms of a licence, please get in touch with me and I'll correct it.

Disclaimer

Every effort has been made to ensure the research distilled into this book is correct, safe and current. We are covering a vast array of topics and mistakes can happen. We are also giving you the bare bones - to let you know the issues and give you coverage on unfamiliar subjects so you can expand your knowledge where needed. If professionals in a speciality contradict this book, follow their lead. If you do things yourself you accept responsibility for problems caused by any lack of knowledge or training on your part.

If you find an error or omission please remember we're a small company. The call to your lawyer will cost you more than I earn in a week, you may be better off just emailing me for a correction :-)

You can contact me at: †††nrtfm.com

ALLi

Proud Member of
The Alliance of Independent Authors
†††<u>Find out more</u>.

Copyright

This content is copyright of
© NRTFM Ltd 2018
All rights reserved.

Any redistribution or reproduction of part or all of the contents in any form is prohibited other than the following:

- you may print or download to a local hard disk extracts for your personal and non-commercial use only
- you may copy the content to individual third parties for their personal use, but only if you acknowledge NRTFM Ltd as the source of the material

You may not, except with our express written permission, distribute or commercially exploit the content. Nor may you transmit it or store it in any other website or other form of electronic retrieval system.

THE END

The End!

71121262R00113

Made in the USA
Middletown, DE
20 April 2018